chilled
cool cocktails

This edition first published in Canada by Whitecap Books
Whitecap Books
351 Lynn Avenue
North Vancouver, BC
V7J 2C4
Phone: 1-888-870-3442

Published by Murdoch Books®, a division of Murdoch Magazines Pty Ltd.

Design Concept: Marylouise Brammer
Designer: Susanne Geppert
Editorial Director: Diana Hill
Editor: Zoë Harpham
Food Director: Lulu Grimes
Cocktails developed by the Murdoch Books Test Kitchen.

Chief Executive: Juliet Rogers
Publisher: Kay Scarlett
Production Manager: Kylie Kirkwood

ISBN 1 55285 428 0

PRINTED IN CHINA by Toppan Printing Co. (HK) Ltd.

Printed 2002.

IMPORTANT: Those who might be at risk from the effects of salmonella food poisoning (the elderly, pregnant
women, young children and those suffering from immune deficiency diseases) should consult their family
doctor with any concerns about eating raw eggs.

chilled
cool cocktails

whitecap

contents

at the bar

For nearly a century, cocktails have epitomised not so much an age, as a style. They have been embraced as a refined way to relax and unwind with friends. The aim of *Chilled* was not only to bring together the classic cocktails, but also to distil from the new contenders those that are sure to become modern classics. The result is a cocktail book for all occasions.

history

Cocktails were popularised during the 1920s when Prohibition in the United States made the production of alcohol illegal. Not surprisingly, this just sent production underground, and illegal, often foul-tasting, bootleg spirits began to be produced. To disguise the flavour and appearance of the bootleg spirits, a wide variety of ingredients were added to them. Since then, the quality of alcohol has improved, but the flavoursome additions have remained popular — many of the classic cocktails come directly from Prohibition days.

equipment

Cocktails are easy to prepare, but having the right equipment will give you the confidence to mix a perfect party drink. The most essential piece of equipment is a cocktail shaker. The standard shaker, widely available in stainless steel, includes a built-in strainer. Another type of shaker, called a Boston shaker, works just as well, but it requires a separate strainer. Another useful piece of equipment is a bar measure (jigger) with 30 ml (1 oz) or 45 ml (1¹/₂ oz) cups to make accurate measuring easy. Once upon a time these two items would be all that you needed, but there is a growing trend to use blenders in cocktail making. Blenders are particularly useful for crushing ice and making some of the fruity, slushy types of cocktails, but in most cases you can make a cocktail just as well by shaking it with some crushed ice. There is a wide range of other cocktail accessories with which to furnish your bar — chopping board, knife, juicer, strainer, wooden muddler, ice bucket, ice scoop, ice tongs, zester, corkscrew, metal strainer, mixing jug, and straws, swizzle sticks and cocktail sticks for garnishes.

glasses

If possible, use glasses that are appropriate to the style of the drink you are serving. Most cocktails are mixed with a certain glass in mind, which in many cases is dictated by tradition. For example, martinis are always served in a martini glass, which comes in standard (100 ml/3¹/₂ oz) and large (150 ml/5 oz) sizes. Although there is an argument for restricting the martini glass to martinis, many people use them for general cocktails as well. Champagne flutes are used for champagne cocktails and some wine cocktails. Old-fashioned glasses or tumblers have a capacity of between 185 ml and 250 ml (6–9 oz) and are used for short mixed drinks and drinks on the rocks. The highball glass is a tall, slim glass used for long drinks, which may be shaken, stirred or built in the glass. It has a capacity of about 290 ml (10 oz). The collins glass is similar to the highball but it was traditionally only used for collinses. Shot glasses are used both for shots and layered shots, and come in 30 ml (1 oz) and 45 ml (1 1/2 oz) sizes. A 400 ml (14 oz) tulip-shaped cocktail glass is used for a variety of mixed and blended drinks, such as daiquiris and piña coladas. In addition, there are wine glasses, goblets, brandy balloons and other specialist glasses, such as the aperitif glass, port or sherry glass and the sour glass (similar to a champagne flute, but with a shorter stem).

sugar syrup Some cocktails may require sugar syrup — it adds the sweetness of sugar and removes the need to dissolve the crystals. To make sugar syrup, combine equal quantities of white sugar and water in a saucepan. Stir to dissolve the sugar, and bring to the boil. Remove from the heat, cool, and store in an airtight bottle in the fridge for up to 3 months.

ice Most cocktails are prepared or served with ice. Ice cubes are ideal for serving or to use in a cocktail shaker; however, crushed ice is better in blended drinks. Crushed ice can be made by wrapping the cubes in a clean tea towel and bashing them with a hammer, or it can be produced in a heavy-duty blender. It can then be stored in the freezer until needed. Have a plentiful supply ready, as most drinks will require the glass or cocktail shaker to be half-full of ice.

bottles
For the home bar, the most important liquors are gin, vodka, brandy, whisky, rum, tequila and vermouth. Just as important are the non-alcoholic components: cola, mineral water (still and sparkling), soda water, tonic water, ginger ale, lemonade, lime juice cordial and cream. Juices are also important: lemon, lime, grapefruit, cranberry, tomato, pineapple, mango and grapefruit — use fresh where possible.

Then there are a whole range of liqueurs, fruit brandies, crèmes, syrups, emulsion liqueurs and whisky liqueurs to choose from. When you're just getting started, buy one or two at a time (in the smallest bottle possible) until you work out which liqueurs you'll use the most.

garnishes
Many of the classic cocktails are identified as much by the garnish as by their ingredients (the Gibson, for example). You'll need at least the traditional ones to get started — maraschino cherries, olives, citrus wedges or twists, and mint. Some cocktails, such as margaritas, require the rim of the glass to be salted. To do this, wipe the rim of the glass with a wedge of lemon or lime, and then dip the rim into a saucer of salt. Press gently, and twist to coat.

Based on the classic Whisky sour, this version has an intriguing almond flavour.

amaretto sour

ice cubes
30 ml (1 oz) amaretto
30 ml (1 oz) lemon juice
30 ml (1 oz) orange juice
maraschino cherry

Half-fill a cocktail shaker with ice. Pour in the amaretto, lemon juice and orange juice and shake well. Strain into a sour glass. Garnish with a cherry.

The Americano is James Bond's *other* favourite cocktail.

americano

ice cubes	Put the ice in a highball glass. Pour over the
30 ml (1 oz) Campari	Campari and vermouth, then top up with
30 ml (1 oz) sweet vermouth	soda water. Garnish with slices of orange
soda water	and lemon and serve with a swizzle stick.
orange slice	
lemon slice	

Bartender's tip	Soda water is purely optional here — many
	people prefer the Americano without it.

If Eve chose a cocktail, this would be it.

apple and calvados champagne cocktail

15 ml ($^1/_2$ oz) Calvados
30 ml (1 oz) clear apple juice
chilled champagne

Pour the Calvados and apple juice into a chilled champagne flute, then carefully top up with champagne.

Bartender's tips

This is one of those rare occasions when fresh isn't best. Freshly squeezed apple juice would cloud this drink; to keep it sparkling, use the bottled variety.
Calvados is an apple brandy made from cider in Normandy.

Don't be deceived by the innocent name — this drink is anything but.

apple blossom

ice cubes
45 ml (1½ oz) apple schnapps
30 ml (1 oz) vodka
15 ml (½ oz) white crème de cacao
45 ml (1½ oz) cream
freshly grated nutmeg

Half-fill a cocktail shaker with ice. Pour in the apple schnapps and vodka, add the crème de cacao and cream, then shake. Strain into a chilled cocktail glass and sprinkle with a little grated nutmeg.

aperitifs

An aperitif is a drink taken before a meal to stimulate the appetite. It's a real French and Italian ritual — an excuse to sit with friends in a bar sipping drinks and nibbling on snacks. The drink can be as simple as a glass of champagne or Campari and soda, or as elegant as a martini.

If this wasn't Noel Coward's cocktail of choice, then it should have been.

b & b

30 ml (1 oz) brandy
30 ml (1 oz) Bénédictine

Pour the brandy and Bénédictine into a warmed brandy balloon or liqueur glass.

Bartender's tip

Warm the brandy balloon before serving for a truly heady aroma.

Named after the B-52 bomber and just as effective.

b-52

15 ml ($^{1}/_{2}$ oz) Kahlúa
15 ml ($^{1}/_{2}$ oz) Irish cream
15 ml ($^{1}/_{2}$ oz) Cointreau

Pour the Kahlúa into a shot glass, then carefully pour the Irish cream over the back of a teaspoon to layer. Clean the spoon, then do the same with the Cointreau to make three distinct layers.

Bartender's tip

You can serve this short or long. Either serve as a shooter or double the quantities of each liqueur and layer them in a brandy balloon. Sip slowly, drinking each layer separately.

The only cocktail to make it to the US supreme court ... protecting it from being made with any other type of rum.

bacardi cocktail

ice cubes
60 ml (2 oz) white Bacardi
30 ml (1 oz) lime or lemon juice
10 ml (¼ oz) grenadine
maraschino cherry

Half-fill a cocktail shaker with ice. Pour in the Bacardi, lime juice and grenadine, then shake. Strain into a chilled cocktail glass. Garnish with a cherry.

Bartender's tip

To get more juice from the lime, roll the fruit between your hands before slicing and squeezing.

Three kinds of rum and a splash of tropical pineapple — perfect for a warm Bahamian night.

bahama mama

ice cubes
15 ml (1/2 oz) Malibu
15 ml (1/2 oz) dark rum
15 ml (1/2 oz) Kahlúa
15 ml (1/2 oz) white rum
crushed ice
pineapple juice
thin pineapple wedge
mint sprig

Half-fill a cocktail shaker with ice. Pour in the Malibu, dark rum, Kahlúa and white rum. Shake well, then strain into a highball glass half-filled with crushed ice. Top up with pineapple juice. Garnish with a thin wedge of pineapple and a small sprig of mint.

When daylight comes, you won't want to go home.

banana bender

1 cup crushed ice
30 ml (1 oz) Cointreau
30 ml (1 oz) banana liqueur
60 ml (2 oz) cream
half a banana, peeled and sliced
maraschino cherry

Combine the ice, Cointreau, banana liqueur, cream and banana in a blender, then blend well. Pour into a champagne flute and garnish with a cherry.

Bartender's tip

Another version of the Banana bender uses half the amount of cream and makes up the difference with pineapple juice.

It's got banana in it, so it must be healthy, right?

banana daiquiri

half a banana, peeled
30 ml (1 oz) white rum
30 ml (1 oz) banana liqueur
30 ml (1 oz) lime juice
15 ml (1/2 oz) sugar syrup
1 cup crushed ice
banana slice

Combine the banana, white rum, banana liqueur, lime juice and sugar syrup in a blender. Blend until smooth, then add the ice and blend until the mixture has the consistency of shaved ice. Pour into a chilled cocktail glass. Garnish with a slice of banana dipped in lemon juice to prevent discoloration.

Inspired by the painter Giovanni Bellini and invented at Harry's Bar in Venice, this drink is a classic.

bellini

30 ml (1 oz) fresh peach nectar
30 ml (1 oz) sugar syrup
chilled prosecco or champagne

Pour the peach nectar and sugar syrup into a chilled champagne flute. Carefully top up with prosecco.

Bartender's tip

Prosecco is an Italian sparkling wine and was the original bubbly in the Bellini. Nowadays, champagne is more common.

This very berry daiquiri captures the essence of summer in a glass.

berry daiquiri

30 ml (1 oz) white rum	Pour the white rum, Cointreau and raspberry
15 ml (1/2 oz) Cointreau	liqueur into a blender, then add the berries.
15 ml (1/2 oz) raspberry liqueur	Blend until smooth, then add the ice and
3 strawberries	blend until the mixture has the consistency of
4 raspberries	shaved ice. Pour the mixture into a chilled
4 blackberries	cocktail glass and garnish with fresh or frozen
1 cup crushed ice	berries on a cocktail stick.
assorted berries	

Bartender's tip   If fresh berries aren't in season, use frozen.

Slip into something more comfortable and slide ...

between the sheets

ice cubes
30 ml (1 oz) white rum
30 ml (1 oz) brandy
30 ml (1 oz) Cointreau
dash of lemon juice
lemon twist

Half-fill a cocktail shaker with ice. Pour in the rum, brandy, Cointreau and lemon juice and shake well. Strain into a chilled cocktail glass and garnish with a twist of lemon.

Come out of the cold and warm up with a Black Russian.

black russian

ice cubes
45 ml (1 1/2 oz) vodka
15 ml (1/2 oz) Kahlúa

Put the ice in an old-fashioned glass, add the vodka and Kahlúa, and stir.

Down to earth Guinness dressed up with champagne — a must for St Patrick's Day.

black velvet

chilled Guinness
chilled champagne

Half-fill a champagne flute with Guinness, then carefully top up with champagne. Don't stir.

Perfect for a summer evening on the back porch.

blackberry spritzer

ice cubes
30 ml (1 oz) Grand Marnier
15 ml (1/2 oz) crème de cassis
10 ml (1/4 oz) lemon juice
6 blackberries
soda water

Half-fill a highball glass with ice and pour in the Grand Marnier, crème de cassis and lemon juice. Add the blackberries and top up with soda water.

blending cocktails

A blended drink is simply ice, flavouring and alcohol blitzed by a blender, with frozen fruit daiquiris being among the most famous (and delicious) examples.

Don't waste your money on a lightweight model blender, because they don't process ice very well. Go for a heavy-duty one — you won't regret it.

For the smoothest result, use pre-crushed ice.

When you wake up at midday, you'll need a little pick-me-up.

bloody mary

3 ice cubes
45 ml (1½ oz) vodka
4 drops of Tabasco
1 teaspoon Worcestershire sauce
10 ml (¼ oz) lemon juice
pinch of salt
grind of black pepper
60 ml (2 oz) chilled tomato juice
1 fresh celery stick

Place the ice cubes in a highball glass, pour in the vodka, then add the Tabasco, Worcestershire sauce and lemon juice. Add the salt and pepper, then pour in the tomato juice and stir well. Allow to sit for a minute and then garnish with a crisp stalk of celery and hope that you will soon feel as fresh.

A favourite from the 1920s cocktail era, a Brandy Alexander is a perfect after-dinner treat.

brandy alexander

ice cubes	Half-fill a cocktail shaker with ice. Pour in the
30 ml (1 oz) brandy	brandy, crème de cacao and cream, and shake
30 ml (1 oz) brown crème de cacao	well to combine. Strain into a chilled cocktail
30 ml (1 oz) cream	glass and dust with nutmeg grated over two
freshly grated nutmeg	crossed straws.
Bartender's tip	Some people like to double the amount
	of cream in this drink. If you're one of
	them, you'll need a slightly larger glass
	to accommodate this added luxury.

An oldie but a goody ... don't just save it for Christmas.

brandy eggnog

ice cubes	Half-fill a cocktail shaker with ice. Pour in the
30 ml (1 oz) brandy	brandy, sugar syrup and egg yolk, and shake
1 teaspoon sugar syrup	well. Strain into a highball glass filled with
1 egg yolk	ice, and top up with milk. Sprinkle with a
milk	little grated nutmeg.
freshly grated nutmeg	

A summer drink — long, cool and refreshing.

brandy, lime and soda

ice cubes
30 ml (1 oz) brandy
15 ml (1/2 oz) lime juice
soda water
dash of lime juice cordial
lime twist

Half-fill a highball glass with ice. Pour in the brandy and lime juice. Top with soda water, then add the lime juice cordial. Garnish with a twist of lime.

Bartender's tip

To keep the soda sparkling and clear, the cordial is added last. It's heavier than soda, so will slowly sink, which minimises stirring.

brandy

Brandy is a spirit distilled from wine. The major difference between brandy and other liquors is that brandy is distilled from fruit instead of grain (whisky) or sugar cane or molasses (rum). If a fruit other than grape is the source, the brandy is named after the parent fruit — one example is cherry brandy. Cognac and armagnac are top-shelf brandies and are only occasionally used in cocktails.

Don't be misled by this drink's sour name — tangy would be more apt.

brandy sour

ice cubes
30 ml (1 oz) brandy
30 ml (1 oz) lemon juice
15 ml (¹/₂ oz) sugar syrup
maraschino cherry

Half-fill a cocktail shaker with ice. Pour in the brandy, lemon juice and sugar syrup, then strain into a chilled sour glass. Garnish with a cherry.

A double shot of spirits will make the meekest person brave.

brave bull

ice cubes	Half-fill an old-fashioned glass with ice. Pour
30 ml (1 oz) Kahlúa	in the Kahlúa, then add the tequila. Swirl
45 ml (1¹/₂ oz) tequila	gently before drinking.

Bartender's tip	For the frothy at heart, you might prefer the creamier version of this drink. Serve it in a sherry glass and top it with a generous twirl of whipped cream.

A drink named after the Bronx zoo is sure to pack a punch.

bronx

ice cubes
30 ml (1 oz) gin
15 ml (1/2 oz) vermouth rosso
15 ml (1/2 oz) dry vermouth
15 ml (1/2 oz) orange juice
strawberry

Half-fill a cocktail shaker with ice. Pour in the gin, vermouth rosso, dry vermouth and orange juice. Shake well, then strain into a cocktail glass. Garnish with a strawberry.

Smooth and creamy, the hint of cinnamon adding the perfect amount of spice.

brown cow

ice cubes
30 ml (1 oz) Tia Maria
60 ml (2 oz) milk
ground cinnamon

Half-fill a cocktail shaker with ice. Pour in the Tia Maria and milk, then shake well. Strain into a cocktail glass. Sprinkle with cinnamon.

Brunch on the balcony, anyone?

buck's fizz

125 ml (4 oz) orange juice
dash of grenadine
chilled champagne
lemon twist

Pour the orange juice and grenadine into a champagne flute. Top slowly with champagne. Garnish with a twist of lemon.

Bartender's tip

You may also know this drink as a Mimosa.

Definitely not one for the faint-hearted!

bullshot

ice cubes
30 ml (1 oz) vodka
30 ml (1 oz) chilled beef stock
10 ml (¼ oz) lemon juice
dash of Worcestershire sauce
pinch of salt
grind of pepper
lemon slice

Half-fill a highball glass with ice, then pour in the vodka, stock, lemon juice and Worcestershire sauce. Add the salt and pepper and stir well. Garnish with a slice of lemon.

building cocktails

The simplest way to make a cocktail is in the glass — this is called 'building' a drink.

No special equipment is needed. Simply pour or 'build' the ingredients over ice in the right serving glass.

Made with the fiery national spirit of Brazil and muddled with lime, this is the cocktail of a new generation.

caipirinha

4 lime wedges 2 sugar cubes 60 ml (2 oz) cachaça crushed ice mint sprig	Put the lime wedges and sugar in an old-fashioned glass and then press well with a wooden spoon or muddler until the limes are crushed. Pour in the cachaça, then stir. Fill with crushed ice and stir again. Garnish with a sprig of mint.
Bartender's tip	A similar drink uses 45 ml (1½ oz) white rum instead of cachaça — it's called a Caipirissima.

Vodka goes Brazilian in this variation on the Caipirinha.

caipiroska

4 lime wedges 10 ml (¼ oz) sugar syrup ice cubes 45 ml (1½ oz) vodka mint sprig	Place the lime wedges in a cocktail shaker with the sugar syrup, and squash down with a wooden spoon or muddler until the limes are crushed. Add the ice cubes to one-third fill the shaker, and pour in the vodka. Shake well and strain into an old-fashioned glass half-full of ice. Garnish with a sprig of mint.
Bartender's tip	For a mintier flavour, add 8 mint leaves and crush them with the limes and sugar syrup.

cachaça

Cachaça (ka-shah-sah) is the national spirit of Brazil. It is also known as caxaca, casa or chacha. Unlike rum, which is distilled from molasses, cachaça is distilled directly from the juice of sugar cane. Technically a brandy, it is also a close cousin to Italian grappa. It has an inimitable burnt sugar flavour closer to rum than to brandy.

Tall, ruby red and very sophisticated.

campari crush

crushed ice
30 ml (1 oz) gin
15 ml (1/2 oz) Campari
ruby red grapefruit juice
lime wedge

Fill a highball glass with crushed ice. Pour in the gin and Campari, then top up with grapefruit juice. Squeeze a wedge of lime into the drink and add the squeezed wedge to the glass.

Make your own sunset with a Campari orange.

campari orange

ice cubes	Half-fill an old-fashioned glass with ice. Pour
45 ml (1½ oz) Campari	in the Campari, then fill with orange juice.
orange juice	Stir well. Garnish with a slice of orange.
orange slice	

campari

Campari is a very bitter Italian liqueur made from quinine and herbs, and it is one of the classic aperitifs. Instantly recognisable by its splash of vivid red colour, it is something of an acquired taste — the Italians say you have to drink it three times before you like it. During Prohibition, Campari was classified as a legal medicinal product, so Americans visiting Italy brought it back by the case load.

A liquid shot of sweet energy — great for après-ski.

caramel bud

ice cubes
30 ml (1 oz) butterscotch schnapps
15 ml (1/2 oz) chocolate liqueur
15 ml (1/2 oz) white crème de cacao
30 ml (1 oz) cream
grated chocolate

Half-fill a cocktail shaker with ice. Pour in the butterscotch schnapps, chocolate liqueur, crème de cacao and cream. Shake and then strain into a chilled cocktail glass. Garnish with grated chocolate.

A grown-up version of your favourite childhood dessert.

champagne and lychee jelly shot

1 gelatine leaf
30 ml (1 oz) sugar syrup
125 ml (4 oz) champagne
3 lychees
6 raspberries

Soak the gelatine in cold water. Heat the sugar syrup and champagne until just hot. Squeeze the liquid out of the gelatine, add to the champagne mixture and stir until dissolved. Cool, then place half a lychee and a raspberry into each of six shot glasses and pour in the champagne mixture. Refrigerate for 3 hours, or until set. Makes six.

champagne cocktails

The champagne cocktail has resisted the fads of fashion throughout the twentieth century and beyond. It is perfect served as an aperitif, or for elegant occasions during the day.

Champagne is the most famous French sparkling wine, and is protected by law. Only wine that is produced in a strictly defined area in France using the *méthode champenoise* may be labelled with the name champagne.

The original (and the best) of the champagne cocktails.

champagne cocktail

1 sugar cube
dash of Angostura bitters
15 ml (1/2 oz) brandy
chilled champagne

Place the sugar cube in a champagne flute. Add the bitters, then the brandy. Slowly top with champagne.

A flavour explosion guaranteed to knock your socks off!

cherry bombe

ice cubes
30 ml (1 oz) gin
15 ml (1/2 oz) cherry brandy
15 ml (1/2 oz) lime juice
15 ml (1/2 oz) Cointreau
1 teaspoon grenadine
dash of Angostura bitters
pineapple juice
pineapple wedge
pineapple leaves

Half-fill a cocktail shaker with ice. Pour in the gin, cherry brandy, lime juice, Cointreau, grenadine and bitters. Shake well and then strain into a highball glass, half-filled with ice. Top up with pineapple juice and garnish with a wedge of pineapple and a couple of pineapple leaves.

A real thirst-quencher for hot summer days.

cherry fizz

ice cubes
45 ml (1¹/₂ oz) brandy
45 ml (1¹/₂ oz) cherry brandy
45 ml (1¹/₂ oz) lemon juice
soda water
cherry juice

Half-fill a cocktail shaker with ice. Pour in the brandy, cherry brandy and lemon juice. Shake well and then strain into a collins glass half-filled with ice. Top up with soda water and a little cherry juice.

'Kiss kiss darling ...
fancy a Chi chi?'

chi chi

1 cup crushed ice
45 ml (1 1/2 oz) vodka
15 ml (1/2 oz) Malibu
30 ml (1 oz) coconut cream
125 ml (4 oz) pineapple juice
pineapple wedge
strawberry

Combine the ice, vodka, Malibu, coconut cream and pineapple juice in a blender and blend well. Pour into a large goblet. Garnish with a small wedge of fresh pineapple and a strawberry.

Martini purists may scoff, but do you care?

chocotini

50 g (1³/4 oz) chocolate
ice cubes
45 ml (1¹/2 oz) vodka
45 ml (1¹/2 oz) brown crème de cacao

Melt the chocolate in a heatproof bowl over simmering water. Dip the rim of a martini glass in the chocolate, or dot the chocolate around the rim. Chill. Half-fill a cocktail shaker with ice. Pour in the vodka and brown crème de cacao. Shake well and strain into the martini glass.

Drink up before the clock strikes midnight.

cinderella

100 ml (3 1/2 oz) orange juice
100 ml (3 1/2 oz) pineapple juice
20 ml (1/2 oz) lemon juice

Combine the orange juice, pineapple juice and lemon juice in a large goblet.

Bartender's tip

Serve this drink chilled. If your juices are at room temperature, shake the drink in an ice-filled shaker before serving.

A couple of these will bring a glow to anyone's cheeks.

citrus blush

ice cubes
15 ml (1/2 oz) lime juice
15 ml (1/2 oz) Limoncello
45 ml (11/2 oz) gin
cranberry juice
lime wedge

Half-fill an old-fashioned glass with ice. Pour in the lime juice, Limoncello and gin. Stir well to combine, top up with cranberry juice, then garnish with a wedge of lime.

Bronzed bodies, bikinis, banana lounges and a Coco colada for good measure.

coco colada

45 ml (1½ oz) brown crème de cacao
125 ml (4 oz) pineapple juice
45 ml (1½ oz) coconut cream
1 cup crushed ice
pineapple wedge

Blend the crème de cacao, pineapple juice and coconut cream together with crushed ice until smooth. Garnish with a wedge of pineapple.

coladas

Coladas may not be one of the true classic cocktails, but who's keeping tabs? They are certainly top of the holiday cocktail list. Basic ingredients of rum, pineapple juice and coconut cream evoke sea breezes and the taste of the tropics. Most famous of the coladas is the Piña colada.

A novel twist on an Irish coffee.

coffee jelly shot

1¹/₂ leaves gelatine
60 ml (2 oz) hot coffee
80 ml (2¹/₂ oz) Tia Maria
15 ml (¹/₂ oz) sugar syrup
whipped cream
grated chocolate

Soak the gelatine in cold water for about 1 minute, or until soft. Squeeze the liquid out of the gelatine and add to the hot coffee. Stir until dissolved. Cool, then add the Tia Maria and sugar syrup, and pour into six shot glasses. Before serving, top with a dollop of whipped cream and sprinkle with grated chocolate. Refrigerate for 3 hours, or until set. Makes six.

For a swank, suave and seductive libation, you can't beat a Continental.

continental

10 ml (1/4 oz) lime juice
1/2 teaspoon sugar
45 ml (1 1/2 oz) white rum
crushed ice
15 ml (1/2 oz) green crème de menthe

Mix the lime juice with the sugar and white rum in an old-fashioned glass, stirring until the sugar dissolves. Half-fill the glass with crushed ice and pour in the crème de menthe. Stir gently to combine.

collinses

Collinses are tall drinks perfect for quenching a thirst with their interplay of sour (lemon), sweet (sugar), bite (liquor) and a bit of bubble (soda water). Similar to a fizz, they are stirred in a collins glass and usually garnished with a lemon wedge and cherry.

A Fantasy Island concoction for wild tropical nights.

copacabana punch

80 ml (2¹/₂ oz) gin
80 ml (2¹/₂ oz) white rum
455 ml (16 oz) champagne
1 litre (35 oz) pineapple juice
quarter of a pineapple, diced
3 passion fruit
20 mint leaves

Pour the gin, white rum, champagne and pineapple juice into a large jug or punch bowl. Add the diced pineapple, passion fruit pulp and mint leaves. Add ice cubes to fill the jug, stir gently to combine and serve in chilled glasses. Serves 10.

Strong enough to raise the dead and keep them partying.

corpse reviver

ice cubes
30 ml (1 oz) brandy
15 ml (1/2 oz) Calvados
15 ml (1/2 oz) sweet vermouth
lemon twist

Half-fill a cocktail shaker with ice. Pour in the brandy, Calvados and vermouth, then shake well. Strain into a martini glass. Garnish with a twist of lemon.

The most urbane of drinks for gorgeous thirty-somethings.

cosmopolitan

ice cubes
30 ml (1 oz) citrus-flavoured vodka
15 ml (1/2 oz) Cointreau
45 ml (11/2 oz) cranberry juice
10 ml (1/4 oz) lime juice
lime twist

Half-fill a cocktail shaker with ice. Pour in the vodka, Cointreau, cranberry juice and lime juice, and shake well. Strain into a large, chilled martini glass. Garnish with a twist of lime.

No diamonds? Sparkle with a drink in your hand instead.

cranberry and vodka sparkle

ice cubes
125 ml (4 oz) cranberry juice
125 ml (4 oz) lemonade or mineral water
10 ml (1/4 oz) lime juice
30 ml (1 oz) vodka

Half-fill a mixing jug with ice. Pour in the cranberry juice, lemonade, lime juice and vodka, then stir. Pour into a highball glass.

Toast the West Indies with this revolutionary formula made famous by the Andrews Sisters' song 'Rum and Coca-cola'.

cuba libre

ice cubes	Half-fill a highball glass with ice. Pour in the
60 ml (2 oz) white rum	rum, squeeze the wedge of lime into the
lime wedge	drink, then add the squeezed wedge to the
cola	glass. Top up with cola.

Reputed to have been inspired by Hemingway, this is a truly cool drink.

daiquiri (frozen)

1 cup crushed ice
60 ml (2 oz) white rum
30 ml (1 oz) lime juice
10 ml (1/4 oz) sugar syrup
lime twist

Combine the ice, rum, lime juice and sugar syrup in a blender. Blend until the mixture has the consistency of shaved ice, then pour into a chilled cocktail glass. Garnish with a twist of lime.

daiquiris

A favourite of both Ernest Hemingway and JFK, the daiquiri still entices. At their simplest, daiquiris consist of white rum, lime juice and sugar syrup. However fruitier, frozen versions of the daiquiri have become popular. Some purists malign the flavoured frozen versions as mere frozen slushies, but when done well they are fruity delights.

Join JFK in his favourite after-work tipple.

daiquiri (shaken)

ice cubes
60 ml (2 oz) white rum
30 ml (1 oz) lime juice
10 ml (¼ oz) sugar syrup

Half-fill a cocktail shaker with ice. Pour in the white rum, lime juice and sugar syrup. Shake vigorously until well mixed and then strain into a chilled cocktail glass.

More than a cocktail, the dry martini is an institution.

dry martini

ice cubes
45 ml (1^1/$_2$ oz) gin
15 ml (^{1}/$_2$ oz) dry vermouth
green olives or a lemon twist

Half-fill a mixing glass with ice. Pour in the gin and vermouth, then stir. Strain into a chilled martini glass and garnish with green olives or a twist of lemon.

Bartender's tip

The amount of vermouth in a martini is a matter of fierce debate, but the trend has been to use less and less. If you are preparing martinis for aficionados, save hassle by asking how they like theirs.

digestifs

After a good meal, there's nothing better than a digestif (simply, an after-dinner drink). There are two main types of digestifs: mixed spirits, and more creamy, complicated concoctions that could almost take the place of dessert.

There is a third kind of digestif, but it is no longer seen very often. It is a *pousse-café* (literally 'coffee pusher' in French), which is a layered drink meant to be sipped slowly, layer by layer.

Gather around a roaring fire with the gang and toast the good old days.

eggnog punch

5 eggs, separated
300 g (10 1/2 oz) sugar
250 ml (9 oz) bourbon
250 ml (9 oz) cream
200 ml (7 oz) milk
freshly grated nutmeg

Whisk the egg whites until stiff, then slowly add 5 tablespoons of the sugar, whisking until glossy. In a large serving bowl, beat the egg yolks with 5 tablespoons of sugar until the sugar has dissolved. Slowly add the bourbon, whisking well. Lightly whisk the cream with the rest of the sugar until the sugar has dissolved. Gently fold the egg whites into the yolk mix, then fold in the cream. Slowly stir in the milk, then chill for 4 hours. Serve each glass dusted with nutmeg. Serves 10.

Give in to your devilish side and order an El diablo.

el diablo

ice cubes	Half-fill a collins glass with ice, pour in
60 ml (2 oz) tequila	the tequila and crème de cassis, then top up
10 ml ($^1/_4$ oz) crème de cassis	with ginger ale. Squeeze the wedge of lime
ginger ale	into the drink, add the squeezed wedge to
lime wedge	the glass. Stir.

eggnogs/flips

The main ingredients of eggnogs and flips are egg yolk, sweetener and spirit — and milk or cream for eggnogs, none for flips. They are well shaken and then served in a cocktail glass, usually with a sprinkling of nutmeg on top. It's worth using freshly grated nutmeg — the fragrance and taste are lively and fresh.

Enjoy this Caribbean classic,
a favourite of 'Americanos'
visiting Cuba during Prohibition.

el presidente

ice cubes	Half-fill a mixing glass with ice. Pour in
30 ml (1 oz) white rum	the rum, vermouth, grenadine and curaçao.
15 ml (1/2 oz) dry vermouth	Stir with ice and then strain into a chilled
1 teaspoon grenadine	cocktail glass.
dash of curaçao	

Indulge the green-eyed monster.

envy

ice cubes
30 ml (1 oz) white rum
15 ml (1/2 oz) amaretto
15 ml (1/2 oz) blue curaçao
15 ml (1/2 oz) lime juice
80 ml (2 1/2 oz) pineapple juice
pineapple wedge

Half-fill a cocktail shaker with ice. Pour in the rum, amaretto, curaçao, lime juice and pineapple juice. Shake well and then strain into a highball glass, half-filled with ice. Garnish with a wedge of pineapple.

Make a date with the devil.

fallen angel

ice cubes
45 ml (1¹/₂ oz) gin
15 ml (¹/₂ oz) green crème de menthe
30 ml (1 oz) lemon juice
dash of Angostura bitters
maraschino cherry

Half-fill a cocktail shaker with ice. Pour in the gin, crème de menthe, lemon juice and bitters, then shake. Strain into a cocktail glass and garnish with a cherry.

This cute and cuddly cocktail has an alcoholic dark side.

fluffy duck

ice cubes
30 ml (1 oz) advocaat
30 ml (1 oz) gin
15 ml (½ oz) Cointreau
30 ml (1 oz) orange juice
30 ml (1 oz) cream
lemonade

Half-fill a highball glass with ice. Pour in the advocaat, gin, Cointreau, orange juice and cream and then top up with lemonade.

fizzes

Essentially, a fizz is a sour with the added effervescence of soda water. But unlike sours, not all fizzes use sugar as their sweetener — syrup or honey are often used instead. Fizzes are usually made from gin, but there are variations using other liquors. Served in an ice-filled collins or highball glass, fizzes are long, cool and refreshing, perfect for a hot summer day.

Pop another record on the hi-fi, sit back and finish the evening with this creamy, seductive concoction.

frankie

ice cubes
30 ml (1 oz) Frangelico
30 ml (1 oz) Kahlúa
30 ml (1 oz) Irish cream
30 ml (1 oz) cream
crushed hazelnuts

Half-fill a cocktail shaker with ice. Pour in the Frangelico, Kahlúa, Irish cream and cream. Shake well, then strain into a large, chilled cocktail glass. Serve sprinkled with very finely crushed hazelnuts.

When the cocktail cupboard is bare, don't despair. You can use any liqueur you have on hand to make a frappé.

frappé

finely crushed ice
30 ml (1 oz) Parfait Amour
15 ml (1/2 oz) Cointreau

Slightly overfill a cocktail glass with crushed ice. Pour over the Parfait Amour and Cointreau. Stir gently and then serve immediately with a short straw.

Bartender's tip

Some classic frappés use Cointreau, crème de menthe or a combination of Midori and Cointreau. Generally, a total of 30 ml (1 oz) liqueur is enough, but if you're like us you won't be able to resist adding a bit more.

In WWI, French officers drank this before battle. It's still good for providing courage.

french 75

ice cubes	Half-fill a cocktail shaker with ice. Pour in the
30 ml (1 oz) gin	gin, lemon juice and sugar syrup and shake
30 ml (1 oz) lemon juice	well. Strain into a highball glass. Add a few
15 ml (1/2 oz) sugar syrup	cubes of ice, then top up with champagne.
chilled champagne	
Bartender's tip	Pour the champagne slowly so you don't lose any sparkle.

The French connection is tenuous, but who cares?

french connection

ice cubes	Half-fill an old-fashioned glass with ice. Pour
30 ml (1 oz) cognac	in the cognac, then the amaretto. Stir well.
15 ml (^{1}/2 oz) amaretto	

The cocktail equivalent of an ice cream to satisfy your inner child.

frozen splice

15 ml ($1/2$ oz) melon liqueur
15 ml ($1/2$ oz) white rum
15 ml ($1/2$ oz) Malibu
15 ml ($1/2$ oz) coconut cream
30 ml (1 oz) pineapple juice
1 cup crushed ice
pineapple wedge
pineapple leaves

Pour the melon liqueur, rum, Malibu, coconut cream and pineapple juice into a blender. Add the crushed ice and blend until smooth. Pour into a large, chilled martini glass. Garnish with a wedge of pineapple and pineapple leaves.

A seductive blend of coffee, cream and Kahlúa to finish off the night.

full moon

ice cubes
30 ml (1 oz) white rum
30 ml (1 oz) Kahlúa
1 teaspoon sugar
pinch of ground cloves
pinch of ground cinnamon
150 ml (5 oz) cold espresso coffee
30 ml (1 oz) cream

Three-quarters fill a highball glass with ice, pour in the rum and Kahlúa, and add the sugar. Stir well until the sugar has dissolved, then add the cloves and cinnamon, and top up with the coffee. Float the cream over the top by carefully pouring it over the back of a teaspoon.

The drink that unified Italy.

garibaldi

ice cubes
45 ml (1¹/₂ oz) Campari
orange juice
half an orange slice

Half-fill a highball glass with ice, pour in the Campari and then the orange juice. Garnish with a half slice of orange.

A martini by another name —
the difference is the briney
flavour of a pearl onion or two.

gibson

ice cubes	Half-fill a mixing glass with ice. Pour in the
60 ml (2 oz) gin	gin and vermouth, then stir. Strain into a
1 teaspoon dry vermouth	chilled martini glass and garnish with a pearl
pearl onions	onion or two.

An old English navy drink that became popular in the USA when fictional sleuth Phillip Marlowe made it his drink.

gimlet

ice cubes
60 ml (2 oz) gin
30 ml (1 oz) lime juice cordial
lime twist

Half-fill a mixing glass with ice, pour in the gin and lime juice cordial and stir well. Strain into a chilled cocktail glass and garnish with a twist of lime.

Bartender's tip

It's worth noting here that by lime juice cordial we mean the thick syrupy cordial from real limes. The kid's version — lurid green, sickly sweet and with little resemblance to real fruit — will ruin any cocktail.

The other European Union.

gin and french

ice cubes
45 ml (1½ oz) gin
30 ml (1 oz) dry French vermouth
lemon twist

Half-fill a mixing glass with ice. Pour in the gin and vermouth and then stir. Strain into a chilled cocktail glass. Garnish with a twist of lemon.

The classic combination of gin and Italian vermouth.

gin and it

ice cubes
45 ml (1¹/2 oz) gin
15 ml (¹/2 oz) vermouth rosso
maraschino cherry

Half-fill a mixing glass with ice. Pour in the gin and vermouth and then stir. Strain into a cocktail glass and garnish with a cherry.

Bartender's tip

Some versions of this recipe served the drink unchilled. It is prepared in its serving glass without ice.

Uncover the inner glamourpuss with a Gin fizz or two.

gin fizz

ice cubes
30 ml (1 oz) gin
15 ml (1/2 oz) lemon juice
10 ml (1/4 oz) sugar syrup
soda water
lemon wedge

Half-fill a cocktail shaker with ice. Pour in the gin, lemon juice and sugar syrup, then shake well. Strain into a highball glass, half-filled with ice, then top up with soda water. Garnish with a small wedge of lemon.

gin

Once known as 'mother's ruin', gin was a cheap liquor that was the scourge of eighteenth-century British mothers. Once controls on distillation were established, gin had a change in fortune and it has now become a popular bar liquor with its herby, juniper bouquet.

There are two main varieties of gin. London dry gin is the one usually used in cocktail-making, while Dutch gin (Genever) is usually served neat because of its strong flavour.

Put your gin to good use and serve this straight up on a hot day.

gin sling

ice cubes
45 ml (1¹/2 oz) gin
30 ml (1 oz) lemon juice
dash of grenadine (optional)
10 ml (¹/4 oz) sugar syrup
soda water

Half-fill an old-fashioned glass with ice. Add the gin, lemon juice, grenadine and sugar syrup and then top up with soda water. Garnish with a cocktail umbrella.

The amaretto really highlights the hint of heather in the Scotch.

godfather

ice cubes	Half-fill an old-fashioned glass with ice. Pour
45 ml (1 1/2 oz) Scotch whisky	in the whisky and amaretto. Stir gently and
20 ml (1/2 oz) amaretto	then serve.

A fairy godmother to make all your dreams come true.

godmother

ice cubes	Half-fill an old-fashioned glass with ice. Pour
45 ml (1^1/2 oz) vodka	in the vodka and amaretto. Stir gently and
20 ml (^{1}/2 oz) amaretto	then serve.

Don't drive ... steer this little number instead.

golden cadillac

ice cubes	Half-fill a cocktail shaker with ice. Pour in the
30 ml (1 oz) Galliano	Galliano, crème de cacao and cream. Shake
30 ml (1 oz) white crème de cacao	well, then strain into a cocktail glass.
30 ml (1 oz) fresh cream	

Silk pyjamas, fluffy slippers and gorgeously plump cushions ... oops, it's only midday.

golden dream

ice cubes
30 ml (1 oz) Galliano
30 ml (1 oz) Cointreau
30 ml (1 oz) orange juice
30 ml (1 oz) cream
orange twist

Half-fill a cocktail shaker with ice. Pour in the Galliano, Cointreau, orange juice and cream. Shake well and then strain into a large, chilled cocktail glass. Garnish with a twist of orange.

A light, fizzy kind of cocktail not to be taken too seriously.

golden fizz

ice cubes
30 ml (1 oz) gin
30 ml (1 oz) lemon juice
15 ml (1/2 oz) sugar syrup
1 egg yolk
soda water

Half-fill a cocktail shaker with ice. Pour in the gin, lemon juice, sugar syrup and egg yolk, then shake well. Strain into a highball glass, half-filled with ice, then top up with soda water.

Grand Marnier and orange add a golden glow to the silvery sheen of a straight margarita.

golden margarita

1 cup crushed ice	Combine the crushed ice, tequila, Grand Marnier, orange juice and lime juice in a blender. Blend until the mixture has the consistency of shaved ice, then pour into a salt-frosted cocktail glass. Garnish with a twist of orange.
30 ml (1 oz) golden tequila	
30 ml (1 oz) Grand Marnier	
30 ml (1 oz) orange juice	
30 ml (1 oz) lime juice	
orange twist	

Bartender's tip	This drink uses golden tequila because of its full, round flavour.

Four words sum up this drink — dessert in a glass.

grasshopper

ice cubes
30 ml (1 oz) green crème de menthe
30 ml (1 oz) white crème de cacao
60 ml (2 oz) cream
grated chocolate

Half-fill a cocktail shaker with ice. Pour in the crème de menthe, crème de cacao and cream. Shake well and strain into a chilled martini glass. Garnish with grated chocolate.

The story goes that a surfer named Harvey loved this drink so much that he kept walking into walls.

harvey wallbanger

crushed ice
30 ml (1 oz) vodka
10 ml (1/4 oz) Galliano
orange juice
orange twist

Half-fill a highball glass with crushed ice. Add the vodka and Galliano, then top up with orange juice. Garnish with a twist of orange.

You've got no cigars, but at least there's no embargo on the Havana special.

havana special

ice cubes
60 ml (2 oz) pineapple juice
10 ml (1/4 oz) cherry brandy
45 ml (1 1/2 oz) white rum
maraschino cherry

Half-fill a cocktail shaker with ice. Pour in the pineapple juice, cherry brandy and rum. Shake well, then strain into a cocktail glass half-filled with ice. Garnish with a cherry.

highballs

A highball is a measure of spirit topped up with ginger ale or soda and served with ice. It is served either in a collins glass or in its own glass, called a highball glass, both of which are tall and elegant. A twist of lemon or orange is the extent of the garnish.

You don't need any fancy bartending skills to make these, just a nice tall glass.

highball

ice cubes
45 ml (1¹/2 oz) whisky
soda water or ginger ale
lemon twist

Half-fill a highball glass with ice cubes. Pour in the whisky and top up with soda water or ginger ale. Garnish with a twist of lemon.

Bartender's tip

A well-known version of the highball uses bourbon and ginger ale in the same quantities as above.

A more sophisticated version of the original backwoods drink.

horse's neck

ice cubes
45 ml (1¹/₂ oz) brandy
1 teaspoon Angostura bitters
ginger ale
1 lemon

Fill a highball glass with ice, then pour in the brandy, then the bitters. Top with ginger ale. Garnish with a 'horse's head'. To make a horse's head, peel away the skin of a lemon in one long piece. Tie a knot in one end. Drape the knotted end of the peel over the inside edge of a highball glass, so that most of the peel dangles outside the glass.

Now you see it, now you don't.

illusion

ice cubes
30 ml (1 oz) melon liqueur
30 ml (1 oz) Cointreau
30 ml (1 oz) vodka
30 ml (1 oz) lemon juice
30 ml (1 oz) pineapple juice
pineapple leaves

Half-fill a cocktail shaker with ice. Pour in the melon liqueur, Cointreau, vodka, lemon juice and pineapple juice. Shake well and then strain into a large, chilled cocktail glass. Garnish with pineapple leaves.

Chocolate and orange show why they are such a winning combination.

jaffa

ice cubes
30 ml (1 oz) Kahlúa
15 ml (1/2 oz) Scotch whisky
15 ml (1/2 oz) Grand Marnier
15 ml (1/2 oz) orange juice
30 ml (1 oz) cream
shaved chocolate curls
orange twist

Half-fill a cocktail shaker with ice. Pour in the Kahlúa, whisky, Grand Marnier, orange juice and cream. Shake well and strain into a chilled cocktail glass. Garnish with shaved chocolate curls and a twist of orange.

Japanese melon liqueur adds a splash of colour to eggnog.

japanese eggnog

ice cubes
45 ml (1½ oz) Cointreau
45 ml (1½ oz) melon liqueur
80 ml (2½ oz) milk
dash of egg white

Half-fill a cocktail shaker with ice. Pour in the Cointreau, melon liqueur, milk and egg white, then shake well. Strain into a cocktail glass.

Elegant, exotic and slightly mysterious. A paper parasol is the ideal garnish.

japanese slipper

ice cubes
30 ml (1 oz) melon liqueur
30 ml (1 oz) Cointreau
30 ml (1 oz) lemon juice
lemon twist

Half-fill a cocktail shaker with ice. Pour in the melon liqueur, Cointreau and lemon juice. Shake well and strain into a chilled martini glass. Garnish with a twist of lemon.

juleps

Juleps are an American invention, originally conceived to mask the flavour of poor-quality alcohol. Today they are admired for their subtle blend of mint and liquor. Prepared in a drinking glass, a julep is made from liquor, fragrant mint leaves, sugar and ice crushed as fine as snow. Some people remove the mint leaves from the glass, but others leave them in to add fresh green colour. A popular garnish is a mint sprig sprinkled with sugar.

No, no, not for the kiddies.

jelly bean

ice cubes
30 ml (1 oz) Sambuca
10 ml (1/4 oz) raspberry cordial
lemonade
jelly beans

Fill a cocktail glass with ice. Pour in the Sambuca and raspberry cordial, then top up with lemonade. Garnish with jelly beans — they should float on the ice.

Sake isn't often used in cocktails, but here it adds a real edge.

kabuki

60 ml (2 oz) sake
30 ml (1 oz) lime juice cordial
15 ml (1/2 oz) sugar syrup
15 ml (1/2 oz) lime juice
15 ml (1/2 oz) Cointreau
6 ice cubes
lime twist

Put the sake, cordial, sugar syrup, lime juice, Cointreau and ice into a blender. Blend well, and pour into a salt-encrusted glass. Garnish with a twist of lime.

Bartender's tip

By lime juice cordial, we mean the thick, syrupy cordial, not the bright green kid's version.

Well, if you're going down you might as well have a last drink.

kamikaze

ice cubes	Half-fill a cocktail shaker with ice. Pour
30 ml (1 oz) vodka	in the vodka, Cointreau, lemon juice and
30 ml (1 oz) Cointreau	lime juice cordial. Shake well and strain
30 ml (1 oz) lemon juice	into a chilled martini glass. Garnish with
dash of lime juice cordial	a cocktail umbrella.
Bartender's tip	By lime juice cordial, we mean the thick, syrupy
	cordial, not the bright green kid's version.

Green, certainly, but not the least bit froglike — more of a prince in disguise.

kermit

ice cubes	Half-fill a cocktail shaker with ice. Add the
30 ml (1 oz) melon liqueur	melon liqueur, banana liqueur, crème de
30 ml (1 oz) banana liqueur	cacao and cream. Shake well, then strain into
15 ml (1/2 oz) white crème de cacao	a chilled cocktail glass. Garnish with a green
60 ml (2 oz) cream	frog lolly on a cocktail stick or with a cherry.
frog lolly or maraschino cherry	

The cold war might be over, but don't let that stop you.

KGB

30 ml (1 oz) Kahlúa
30 ml (1 oz) Irish cream
30 ml (1 oz) Grand Marnier

Pour the Kahlúa into an old-fashioned glass, then pour the Irish cream over the back of a teaspoon to create a second layer. Repeat with the Grand Marnier so that you have three layers.

Bartender's tip

Layered drinks such as this are now more common as shooters. To make this a shooter, halve the quantities of liqueur and layer in a shot glass.

Don't know what to drink?
A Kir is always a classy choice.

kir

15 ml (1/2 oz) crème de cassis chilled dry white wine	Pour crème de cassis into a wine goblet, then slowly top with chilled white wine.
Bartender's tip	Crème de cassis is a liqueur made from blackcurrants. Some people regard it as a health-giving restorative.

Might as well make a royal occasion of it.

kir royal

2 dashes of crème de cassis
chilled champagne

Pour the crème de cassis into a champagne flute, then slowly top with champagne.

The sweet, acidic tang of kiwi fruit melds perfectly with tequila.

kiwi margarita

crushed ice
45 ml (1½ oz) tequila
30 ml (1 oz) Cointreau
30 ml (1 oz) melon liqueur
30 ml (1 oz) lemon juice
1–2 kiwi fruit, peeled and chopped
kiwi fruit slices

Combine the ice, tequila, Cointreau, melon liqueur, lemon juice and kiwi fruit in a blender and blend well. Pour into a salt-frosted cocktail glass. Garnish with slices of kiwi fruit on a cocktail sticks.

Another variation on the gin–vermouth combination.

knickerbocker

ice cubes
15 ml (¹/₂ oz) dry vermouth
dash of sweet vermouth
30 ml (1 oz) gin
slice of lemon

Fill a mixing glass with ice. Add the dry vermouth, sweet vermouth and gin. Strain into a chilled martini glass. Squeeze a slice of lemon into the drink and add the squeezed slice to the glass.

Try a Flaming Lamborghini — set the chartreuse alight for a few moments before drinking, but watch your eyebrows!

lamborghini

15 ml (1/2 oz) Kahlúa
15 ml (1/2 oz) Galliano
15 ml (1/2 oz) green chartreuse

Pour the Kahlúa into a port or shot glass, then gently pour the Galliano over the back of a teaspoon into the glass to create another layer. Repeat with the chartreuse to create three distinct layers.

layering cocktails

No other drink has the visual impact of a layered drink. Making these drinks requires a bit of luck, but the secret is to first pour the heaviest liquor into a glass, then slowly and steadily pour a less dense liquor over the back of a teaspoon into the glass. Repeat, then admire your work.

Generally, syrupy liqueurs are the most dense, then cream liqueurs and lastly regular spirits, but this varies between brands.

Traditionalists prefer gin in their martinis, but one sip of this could convert them.

lemon drop martini

1 teaspoon sugar
15 ml (1/2 oz) lemon juice
80 ml (2 1/2 oz) vodka
lemon twist

Put the sugar and lemon juice into a cocktail shaker. Stir until the sugar has dissolved, then half-fill the shaker with ice. Add the vodka and shake well. Strain into a chilled martini glass and garnish with a twist of lemon.

When a collins meets a sour, you get a rickey.

lime rickey

ice cubes
45 ml (1¹/2 oz) gin
15 ml (¹/2 oz) sugar syrup
15 ml (¹/2 oz) lime juice
soda water
lime twist
lime slice

Half-fill a highball glass with ice. Add the gin, sugar syrup and lime juice, then top up with soda water. Garnish with a twist of lime and a slice of lime (and a swizzle stick!).

The effervescent tartness of the lemon makes this an ideal aperitif.

limoncello cocktail

10 ml (1/4 oz) lime juice
15 ml (1/2 oz) Limoncello
chilled champagne

Pour the lime juice and Limoncello into a chilled champagne flute and slowly top up with champagne. If the champagne is added too quickly it may fizz up and overflow.

Bartender's tip

Limoncello is a vodka flavoured by a lemon zest infusion, then mixed with a sugar syrup.

This cocktail is much more sophisticated than the sweet-shop name implies.

liquorice allsort

ice cubes
15 ml (¹/2 oz) black Sambuca
15 ml (¹/2 oz) strawberry liqueur
15 ml (¹/2 oz) Malibu
60 ml (2 oz) cream
liquorice allsort

Half-fill a cocktail shaker with ice. Pour in the Sambuca, strawberry liqueur, Malibu and cream and shake well. Strain into a chilled cocktail glass and garnish with a liquorice allsort.

Those days of innocence, sitting on the swing, sipping iced tea ... long gone!

long island iced tea

ice cubes
15 ml (1/2 oz) white rum
15 ml (1/2 oz) vodka
15 ml (1/2 oz) gin
15 ml (1/2 oz) Cointreau
15 ml (1/2 oz) tequila
1/2 teaspoon lime juice
cola
lime wedge

Half-fill a highball glass with ice cubes. Pour in the white rum, vodka, gin, Cointreau, tequila and lime juice, then top up with cola. Stir well with a swizzle stick to combine. Garnish with a wedge of lime.

Created by the famous American bartender Trader Vic to satisfy some home-sick Tahitian friends, a Mai tai still evokes Polynesian paradise.

mai tai

crushed ice
60 ml (2 oz) white rum
30 ml (1 oz) dark rum
15 ml (1/2 oz) Cointreau
15 ml (1/2 oz) amaretto
15 ml (1/2 oz) lemon juice
80 ml (21/2 oz) pineapple juice
100 ml (31/2 oz) orange juice
15 ml (1/2 oz) sugar syrup
dash of grenadine
lime slice and mint leaves

Half-fill a large cocktail glass with crushed ice. Add the white rum, dark rum, Cointreau, amaretto, lemon juice, pineapple juice, orange juice, sugar syrup and grenadine. Stir and then garnish with a slice of lime and a few mint leaves.

The martini has hit new heights with the advent of flavoured vodkas.

mandarini martini

ice cubes	Half-fill a mixing glass with ice. Pour in the
60 ml (2 oz) mandarin vodka	vodka and vermouth. Stir, then strain into a
15 ml (1/2 oz) dry vermouth	chilled martini glass and garnish with a twist
orange twist	of orange.
Bartender's tip	Citrus zesters are the best tool for making
	citrus twists. A zester has holes at one end
	of an angled blade. The blade is run over
	the zest of citrus fruit to produce long, thin
	shreds of zest that are great for a garnish.

The Bellini goes tropical in this delicious variation on an old favourite.

mango bellini

15 ml (1/2 oz) mango juice chilled champagne	Pour the mango juice into a champagne flute and slowly top up with champagne.

One of the all-time favourite fruity cocktails — keep plenty of crushed ice on hand.

mango daiquiri

half a mango, peeled and diced
30 ml (1 oz) white rum
30 ml (1 oz) mango liqueur
30 ml (1 oz) lemon juice
15 ml (1/2 oz) sugar syrup
1 cup crushed ice

Combine the diced mango, rum, mango liqueur, lemon juice and sugar syrup in a blender. Blend until smooth, then add the ice and blend until the mixture has the consistency of shaved ice. Pour into a chilled cocktail glass.

A luscious blend of tropical fruit, decadent cream and delicious liqueurs.

mango tango

30 ml (1 oz) mango liqueur
30 ml (1 oz) Grand Marnier
15 ml ($1/2$ oz) sugar syrup
30 ml (1 oz) cream
30 ml (1 oz) milk
half a mango, diced
8 ice cubes
fresh mango purée

Put the mango liqueur, Grand Marnier, sugar syrup, cream, milk, diced mango and ice into a blender. Blend until the mixture is thick and smooth and then pour into a tall, chilled cocktail glass. Garnish with a swirl of fresh mango purée.

A drink from the golden era of the Manhattan Club in the late nineteenth century.

manhattan

ice cubes	Half-fill a cocktail shaker with ice. Pour in
45 ml (1 1/2 oz) Southern Comfort	the Southern Comfort, vermouth and bitters,
15 ml (1/2 oz) vermouth rosso	then shake well. Strain into a chilled cocktail
dash of Angostura bitters	glass. Garnish with a cherry.
maraschino cherry	

The city has been distilled into the most elegant of drinks.

manhattan dry

ice cubes
45 ml (1 1/2 oz) Southern Comfort
15 ml (1/2 oz) dry vermouth
dash of Angostura bitters
lemon twist

Half-fill a cocktail shaker with ice. Pour in the Southern Comfort, vermouth and bitters, then shake well. Strain into a chilled cocktail glass. Garnish with a twist of lemon.

margaritas

Since its invention in the 1930s or 1940s, the margarita has become the most popular cocktail in the United States. All margaritas are variations on the same theme — tequila, orange liqueur, lime juice, ice and salt. Originally shaken, most margaritas are now blended with crushed ice.

A salt-encrusted rim is an essential component of a margarita. To salt the rim of your glass, smear the rim with a wedge of lemon, then dip the rim into a saucer of salt.

Think cold as ice and keep everything perfectly chilled for the ultimate frozen margarita.

margarita (frozen)

1 cup crushed ice
60 ml (2 oz) tequila
30 ml (1 oz) Cointreau
30 ml (1 oz) lemon juice
lemon wedge

Combine the ice, tequila, Cointreau and lemon juice in a blender. Blend until the mixture resembles shaved ice and pour into a salt-frosted cocktail glass. Garnish with a wedge of lemon.

A margarita in its original form — shaken rather than blitzed in a blender.

margarita (shaken)

ice cubes	Half-fill a cocktail shaker with ice. Pour in
60 ml (2 oz) tequila	the tequila, Cointreau and lemon or lime
30 ml (1 oz) Cointreau	juice, then shake well. Strain into a salt-
30 ml (1 oz) lemon or lime juice	frosted cocktail glass.

The Martinez cocktail is rumoured to be the father of the martini.

martinez cocktail

ice cubes
30 ml (1 oz) gin
30 ml (1 oz) dry vermouth
dash of Angostura bitters
dash of triple sec
maraschino cherry

Half-fill a mixing glass with ice. Pour in the gin, vermouth, bitters and triple sec. Stir well, then strain into a chilled cocktail glass. Garnish with a cherry.

Melon gleams in this twist on the classic margarita.

melon margarita

1 cup crushed ice
30 ml (1 oz) melon liqueur
30 ml (1 oz) tequila
45 ml (1½ oz) lemon juice
15 ml (½ oz) sugar syrup
lemon twist

Combine the ice, melon liqueur, tequila, lemon juice and sugar syrup in a blender. Blend until the mixture resembles shaved ice, then pour into a salt-frosted cocktail glass. Garnish with a twist of lemon.

martinis

As much a status symbol as a drink, the martini continues to bewitch us with its elegance and simplicity. The origin of the martini cannot be definitively placed, except to say that it was invented sometime in America in the late nineteenth century. Originally a simple formula of gin, French vermouth and olives, today there are many variations — considered bastardization by some, ingenuity by others.

Who wants to drink a Millionaire? I do!

millionaire

ice cubes
20 ml (1/2 oz) lemon juice
1 egg white
10 ml (1/4 oz) Cointreau
1 teaspoon grenadine
45 ml (11/2 oz) bourbon

Half-fill a cocktail shaker with ice. Pour in the lemon juice, egg white, Cointreau, grenadine and bourbon. Strain into a sour glass.

A relic of the genteel Virginia society that invented it.

mint julep

4 mint leaves
4 sugar cubes
crushed ice
60 ml (2 oz) bourbon
dash of dark rum or brandy
sprig of mint

Crush the mint leaves and sugar cubes with the back of a wooden spoon or muddler in a large highball glass. Fill with crushed ice, then pour in the bourbon and stir. Top with a dash of rum or brandy. Serve with a long straw and garnish with a sprig of mint.

What's that shimmering on the edge of the bar?

mirage

ice cubes	Fill a highball glass one-third full of ice. Pour in the lime juice, melon liqueur and ginger beer. Mix the vodka and strawberry liqueur in a separate glass, then gently 'float' the vodka mixture onto the ginger beer by pouring it over the back of a teaspoon. Garnish with a slice of lime.
30 ml (1 oz) lime juice	
30 ml (1 oz) melon liqueur	
100 ml (3½ oz) non-alcoholic ginger beer	
30 ml (1 oz) vodka	
15 ml (½ oz) strawberry liqueur	
lime slice	

Meet the Mint julep's very much more exciting cousin.

mojito

2 sprigs of fresh mint
1 teaspoon sugar
45 ml (1¹/2 oz) lime juice
ice cubes
60 ml (2 oz) white rum
soda water

In a highball glass, crush the mint and the sugar together with the end of a wooden spoon or muddler. Add the lime juice, then three-quarters fill the glass with ice. Pour in the white rum and top up with soda.

Bartender's tip

Many people believe that the secret to a great Mojito is to let your squeezed lime bob in the drink. The oils from the zest add a faint bitterness that really enhances the drink.

muddling cocktails

Muddling is a mixing term meaning to stir and mash. It basically involves crushing ingredients (often herbs and fruit) with a pestle (sometimes called a muddler) or the back end of a spoon. The idea is to extract as much flavour as possible from the ingredients. To muddle a drink, put the ingredients in a glass with a tough underside, then crush the ingredients against the bottom of the glass. Mix well, then prepare your cocktail.

Though this drink is traditionally served in a copper mug, a highball glass adds class.

moscow mule

ice cubes	Half-fill a highball glass with ice cubes.
60 ml (2 oz) vodka	Add the vodka and lime juice, then top
15 ml ($^1/_2$ oz) lime juice	up with ginger beer and garnish with a
non-alcoholic ginger beer	wedge of lime.
lime wedge	

Not nearly as dirty as the name implies and far, far tastier.

mudslide

50 g (1³/4 oz) chocolate, melted
ice cubes
30 ml (1 oz) Kahlúa
45 ml (1¹/2 oz) Irish cream
15 ml (¹/2 oz) vodka

Dip the rim of an old-fashioned glass in the melted chocolate to coat the edge. Half-fill the glass with ice. Pour in the Kahlúa, Irish cream and vodka, then stir well.

Bartender's tip

A Mudslide is sometimes made with equal quantities of the three liqueurs — 15 ml (¹/2 oz) of each.

The classic Italian *aperitivo*.

negroni

ice cubes
30 ml (1 oz) gin
30 ml (1 oz) vermouth rosso
30 ml (1 oz) Campari
soda water (optional)
orange twist

Half-fill a mixing glass with ice. Pour in the gin, vermouth and Campari, then stir well. Strain into a cocktail glass. Add a dash of soda water if you like. Garnish with a twist of orange.

Ideal for city slickers and sophisticated urbanites.

new-yorker

ice cubes
45 ml (1¹/₂ oz) bourbon
1 teaspoon lime juice
dash of grenadine
orange twist

Half-fill a cocktail shaker with ice. Pour in the bourbon, lime juice and grenadine, then shake well. Pour into an old-fashioned glass. Garnish with a twist of orange.

One of the greats of cocktail history and perhaps the first all-American cocktail.

old-fashioned

1 sugar cube
dash of Angostura bitters
soda water
ice cubes
60 ml (2 oz) whisky
orange twist

Place the sugar cube into an old-fashioned glass, add the bitters and allow it to absorb into the sugar. Add a splash of soda water and ice to half-fill the glass. Pour in the whisky and stir to dissolve the sugar. Garnish with a twist of orange.

This award-winning cocktail is a stunning pre-dinner drink.

olé

ice cubes
45 ml (1¹/₂ oz) tequila
30 ml (1 oz) banana liqueur
dash of blue curaçao

Half-fill a cocktail shaker with ice. Pour in the tequila and banana liqueur, then shake well. Strain into a liqueur glass. Tip a dash of blue curaçao into the drink to achieve a two-tone effect.

Sure, it looks innocent ... but this is no ordinary jelly.

orange jelly shot

1 gelatine leaf
10 ml (1/4 oz) sugar syrup
60 ml (2 oz) pulp-free orange juice
15 ml (1/2 oz) lemon juice
60 ml (2 oz) Grand Marnier
30 ml (1 oz) Galliano
6 orange segments

Soak the gelatine leaf in cold water. Heat the sugar syrup, orange juice and lemon juice until just hot. Squeeze the liquid out of the gelatine, add to the juice mixture and stir until dissolved. Cool, then add the Grand Marnier and Galliano. Place an orange segment in each of six shot glasses, and pour in the orange mixture. Refrigerate for 3 hours, or until set. Makes six.

Have another.
And another.
And ...

orgasm

ice cubes
30 ml (1 oz) Cointreau
30 ml (1 oz) Irish cream
1 strawberry
2 maraschino cherries

Half-fill an old-fashioned glass with ice. Pour in the Cointreau and Irish cream, and stir to mix. Garnish with a strawberry and a couple of cherries.

Paradise is a cocktail lounge.

paradise

ice cubes
30 ml (1 oz) gin
15 ml (1/2 oz) apricot brandy
1 teaspoon orange juice
half an orange slice
maraschino cherry

Half-fill a cocktail shaker with ice. Pour in the gin, brandy and orange juice and shake well. Strain into a cocktail glass, then garnish with half a slice of orange and a cherry.

A Sunday morning special.

parson's special

ice cubes	Half-fill a cocktail shaker with ice. Pour
60 ml (2 oz) orange juice	in the orange juice, grenadine and egg yolk,
10 ml (1/4 oz) grenadine	then shake well. Strain into an ice-filled
1 egg yolk	highball glass and top with soda water.
soda water	Garnish with a wheel of orange.
orange wheel	

Bartender's tip	A wheel of orange is simply a slice of orange.
	So that it will sit on the rim of the glass, cut
	a slice from the centre to the peel.

The specks of passion fruit seeds look fabulous suspended in the jelly.

passion fruit and vodka jelly shot

1 gelatine leaf
30 ml (1 oz) sugar syrup
60 ml (2 oz) passion fruit pulp
80 ml (2¹/2 oz) vodka

Soak the gelatine leaf in cold water. Heat the sugar syrup and passion fruit pulp until just hot. Squeeze the liquid out of the gelatine, then add to the passion fruit mixture and stir to dissolve. Cool, then stir in the vodka and pour into six shot glasses. Refrigerate for 3 hours, or until set. Makes six.

Drink your way to a peaches and cream complexion.

peach and mint iced tea

1 peach-scented tea bag
8 mint leaves
ice cubes
30 ml (1 oz) white rum
15 ml ($1/2$ oz) peach schnapps
10 ml ($1/4$ oz) sugar syrup
10 ml ($1/4$ oz) lemon juice

Place the tea bag in 125 ml ($1/2$ cup) boiling water. Add 4 mint leaves and leave to infuse for 5 minutes, then discard the tea bag and chill the tea. Remove and discard the mint. Half-fill a highball glass with ice cubes, pour in the peach tea and add the white rum, peach schnapps, sugar syrup, lemon juice and remaining mint leaves. Stir well to combine.

A softer than normal margarita.

peach margarita

30 ml (1 oz) tequila
30 ml (1 oz) peach schnapps
15 ml (½ oz) lime juice
15 ml (½ oz) sugar syrup
1 peach, peeleed, seeded and chopped
1 cup crushed ice
frozen peach cubes

Combine the tequila, peach schnapps, lime juice, sugar syrup and peach in a blender. Blend until smooth, then add the ice and blend until the mixture has the consistency of shaved ice. Pour into a salt-frosted cocktail glass and garnish with frozen peach cubes on a cocktail stick.

This one's for the sentimental at heart.

per f'amour

ice cubes
30 ml (1 oz) Cointreau
15 ml (1/2 oz) Parfait Amour
45 ml (11/2 oz) orange juice
dash of egg white
orange twist

Half-fill a cocktail shaker with ice. Pour in the Cointreau, Parfait Amour, orange juice and egg white. Shake well until frothy, then strain into a chilled martini glass. Garnish with a twist of orange.

A truly sophisticated drink that packs an amazing punch.

perfect martini

ice cubes
60 ml (2 oz) gin
15 ml ($1/2$ oz) dry vermouth
15 ml ($1/2$ oz) sweet vermouth
green olives or lemon twist

Half-fill a mixing glass with ice. Pour in the gin, dry vermouth and sweet vermouth and stir. Strain into a chilled martini glass and garnish with green olives or a twist of lemon.

A perennial favourite at Wimbledon. Anyone for tennis?

pimm's

ice cubes	Half-fill a highball glass with ice. Pour
45 ml (1 1/2 oz) Pimm's No. 1	in the Pimm's. Top up with lemonade and
lemonade	ginger ale in equal quantities. Garnish with
ginger ale	slices of cucumber, orange and lemon.
slice of cucumber skin	
orange slice	
lemon slice	
Bartender's tip	Pimm's No. 1 is gin-based, but you could use
	Pimm's No. 2 (brandy-based) instead.

Refresh the hordes with a generous bowl of Pimm's punch.

pimm's punch

80 ml (2¹/2 oz) orange juice
ice cubes
400 ml (14 oz) Pimm's No. 1
400 ml (14 oz) bourbon
185 ml (6 oz) sweet vermouth
185 ml (6 oz) white rum
290 ml (10 oz) orange juice
1 bottle of champagne
chopped fresh fruit

Freeze the orange juice in an ice-cube tray. Just before you're ready to serve, half-fill a punchbowl with ice, add the Pimm's, bourbon, vermouth, white rum, orange juice and champagne. Stir in the fresh fruit and the frozen orange juice cubes. Serves 10.

Float up to the poolside bar for a Piña colada and a cocktail umbrella to keep off the sun.

piña colada

1 cup crushed ice
45 ml (1¹/2 oz) white rum
30 ml (1 oz) coconut cream
30 ml (1 oz) Malibu
100 ml (3¹/2 oz) pineapple juice
15 ml (¹/2 oz) sugar syrup
pineapple leaves

Combine the ice, rum, coconut cream, Malibu, pineapple juice and sugar syrup in a blender. Blend well until slushy and pour into a large, chilled cocktail glass. Garnish with pineapple leaves and a cocktail umbrella.

A shooter that you can eat.

piña colada jelly shot

1 gelatine leaf
30 ml (1 oz) cream
20 ml (¹/₂ oz) sugar syrup
60 ml (2 oz) pineapple juice
30 ml (1 oz) white rum
30 ml (1 oz) Malibu

Soak the gelatine leaf in cold water. Gently heat the cream with the sugar syrup and pineapple juice until just hot. Squeeze the liquid out of the gelatine, add to the cream mixture and stir until dissolved. Cool, then stir in the white rum and Malibu. Pour into six shot glasses and garnish each with a pineapple leaf. Refrigerate for 3 hours, or until set. Makes six.

Destined to become a modern classic.

pineapple, lychee and mint daiquiri

4 mint leaves
45 ml (1½ oz) white rum
80 g (½ cup) diced, fresh pineapple
4 lychees
15 ml (½ oz) pineapple juice
15 ml (½ oz) lime juice
15 ml (½ oz) sugar syrup
1 cup crushed ice
pineapple leaves

Put the mint leaves, white rum, pineapple, lychees, pineapple juice, lime juice and sugar syrup into a blender. Add the ice and blend until the mixture has the consistency of shaved ice. Pour into a large chilled cocktail glass and garnish with pineapple leaves.

Get the party off to a swinging start with this South American favourite.

pisco sour

ice cubes
45 ml (1 1/2 oz) pisco brandy
20 ml (1/2 oz) lemon juice
10 ml (1/4 oz) sugar syrup
dash of Angostura bitters
dollop of egg white

Half-fill a cocktail shaker with ice. Pour in the pisco, lemon juice, sugar syrup, bitters and egg white, then shake well. Strain into a sour glass or cocktail glass.

Bartender's tip

Pisco is a type of brandy, popular in Chile and Peru. In South America, the Pisco sour is often dusted with cinnamon.

A smooth tropical libation drunk by the plantation owners of Jamaica. Use Jamaican rum for an authentic flavour.

planter's punch

ice cubes
500 ml (17 oz) dark rum
200 ml (7 oz) lime juice
200 ml (7 oz) lemon juice
4 tablespoons caster sugar
1 teaspoon Angostura bitters
500 ml (17 oz) soda water
fresh fruit slices (e.g. kiwi fruit and pineapple)

One-third fill a large punchbowl with ice. Pour in the dark rum, lime juice, lemon juice, sugar and bitters. Mix together, then top up with soda water. Garnish with slices of fresh fruit. Serves 10.

Don't let the fluffy name or appearance deceive you — this is a serious drink.

porto flip

ice cubes
15 ml (1/2 oz) brandy
45 ml (11/2 oz) red port
egg yolk
freshly grated nutmeg

Half-fill a cocktail shaker with ice. Pour in the brandy, port and egg yolk, then shake well. Strain into a cocktail glass. Grate a little nutmeg over the top.

A Bush oyster is a Prairie oyster with a beer chaser — only for the very brave.

prairie oyster

10 ml ($1/2$ oz) Worcestershire sauce
10 ml ($1/2$ oz) tomato sauce
2 drops of Tabasco
egg yolk
good pinch of salt
grind of pepper

Pour the Worcestershire sauce, tomato sauce and the Tabasco into an old-fashioned glass and stir together. Gently add the egg yolk without breaking it. Season with salt and pepper. Swallow in one gulp.

No time for foreplay — get down and dirty with a QF.

QF

15 ml (1/2 oz) Kahlúa
15 ml (1/2 oz) melon liqueur
15 ml (1/2 oz) Irish cream

Layer the Kahlúa, melon liqueur and Irish cream in a shot glass, pouring each liqueur over the back of a teaspoon to achieve three distinct layers.

The quintessential child's drink has now grown up ... well, a little.

raspberry champagne spider

raspberry sorbet chilled champagne	Scoop raspberry sorbet into small balls with a melon baller and freeze until needed. Place one or two balls in a champagne flute and slowly top up with champagne.
Bartender's tip	You can use any flavoured sorbet that you like, or even go multi-coloured.

A classy number, and very beautiful, too.

ritz fizz

dash of blue curaçao
dash of amaretto
dash of lemon juice
chilled champagne

Pour the curaçao, amaretto and lemon juice into a champagne flute and slowly top with champagne.

Bartender's tip

Amaretto is an almond-flavoured liqueur. You could also try crème de cassis, which is a blackcurrant-flavoured liqueur, or Cointreau, which is orange-flavoured.

Head into battle with the courage of a Rob Roy under your kilt.

rob roy

ice cubes
60 ml (2 oz) Scotch whisky
30 ml (1 oz) vermouth rosso
dash of Angostura bitters
maraschino cherry

Half-fill a cocktail shaker with ice. Pour in the whisky, vermouth and bitters, then shake well. Strain into a chilled cocktail glass. Garnish with a cherry.

rum

The darling of the Caribbean, rum is a spirit distilled from fermented sugar cane juice or molasses. There are many styles of rum, each with different characteristics, from nearly colourless and faintly aromatic to deep dark brown and richly flavoured. The colour depends on how and in which vessel the rum was aged. Charred oak casks impart a warm brown colour, whereas stainless steel tanks leave the rum colourless.

Two of Scotland's finest liquors combine in this surprisingly smooth drink.

rusty nail

ice cubes
45 ml (1 1/2 oz) Scotch whisky
45 ml (1 1/2 oz) Drambuie
lemon twist

Half-fill an old-fashioned glass or tumbler with ice. Pour in the whisky and then the Drambuie. Garnish with a twist of lemon.

Bartender's tip

Our recipe uses equal quantities of Scotch whisky and Drambuie. You may prefer to increase the whisky by a half measure for a stronger nightcap.

Oriental mystique meets Western tradition in an intriguing twist on the martini.

saketini

ice cubes
30 ml (1 oz) sake
60 ml (2 oz) vodka
a dash of dry vermouth
shaved cucumber twist

Half-fill a mixing glass with ice. Pour in the sake, vodka and dry vermouth. Stir, then strain into a chilled martini glass and garnish with a twist of shaved cucumber.

Need a stiff drink? Look no further than a Salty dog.

salty dog

ice cubes	Fill a salt-frosted old-fashioned glass with ice.
45 ml (1 1/2 oz) vodka	Pour in the vodka and top up with grapefruit
grapefruit juice	juice. Garnish with a twist of lemon.
lemon twist	
Bartender's tip	To make this a Salty red dog, use ruby red
	grapefruit juice.

The Spanish version of punch, which goes down oh so easily.

sangria

20 ml (1/2 oz) lemon juice
20 ml (1/2 oz) orange juice
1 1/2 tablespoons caster sugar
1 bottle of red wine
570 ml (20 oz) lemonade
45 ml (1 1/2 oz) gin
45 ml (1 1/2 oz) vodka
lemon wheels
orange wheels
lime wheels
ice

Pour the lemon juice, orange juice and sugar into a large jug or bowl and stir until the sugar has dissolved. Add the red wine, lemonade, gin and vodka. Add the fruit and enough ice to fill the jug, then stir and serve. Serves 10.

Take a trip to the wild side.

screaming lizard

20 ml (1/2 oz) green chartreuse 20 ml (1/2 oz) tequila	Pour the chartreuse into a shot glass. Carefully pour the tequila over the back of a spoon to create two distinct layers.
Bartender's tip	For those who like their drinks served cold, shake the chartreuse and tequila in a cocktail shaker with ice, then strain into a shot glass.

Yes! Yes! Yes!

screaming orgasm

ice cubes
30 ml (1 oz) Galliano
30 ml (1 oz) Irish cream
15 ml (1/2 oz) Cointreau
15 ml (1/2 oz) Kahlúa
30 ml (1 oz) cream
strawberry

Half-fill a cocktail shaker with ice. Pour in the Galliano, Irish cream, Cointreau, Kahlúa and cream, then shake well. Strain into a martini glass. Garnish with a strawberry.

Using a screwdriver as a swizzle stick? That's exactly what some oil riggers did ... hence the name.

screwdriver

ice cubes
45 ml (1 1/2 oz) vodka
orange juice
orange twist
maraschino cherry

Half-fill a highball glass with ice. Pour in the vodka and top with orange juice. Garnish with a twist of orange and a cherry and serve with a straw.

An ultra-refreshing cure for work stress, relationship blues or a bad hair day.

seabreeze

ice cubes
60 ml (2 oz) vodka
60 ml (2 oz) cranberry juice
60 ml (2 oz) ruby red grapefruit juice
15 ml (1/2 oz) lime juice
lime twist

Half-fill a cocktail shaker with ice. Pour in the vodka, cranberry juice, grapefruit juice and lime juice. Shake well and strain into a highball glass, half-filled with ice. Garnish with a twist of lime.

The art of seduction involves a spoon.

seduction

15 ml (1/2 oz) Kahlúa
15 ml (1/2 oz) melon liqueur
15 ml (1/2 oz) Irish cream

Pour the Kahlúa into a shot glass. Carefully pour the melon liqueur, then the Irish cream over the back of a spoon so that you have three distinct layers.

Even better than the reality — there's no gritty sand to contend with.

sex on the beach

ice cubes
45 ml (1¹/₂ oz) vodka
30 ml (1 oz) peach schnapps
45 ml (1¹/₂ oz) pineapple juice
45 ml (1¹/₂ oz) cranberry juice
crushed ice

Half-fill a cocktail shaker with ice. Pour in the vodka, schnapps, pineapple juice and cranberry juice and shake well. Strain into a tall cocktail glass, half-filled with crushed ice.

shaking cocktails

To shake a cocktail, half-fill a cocktail shaker with ice, pour in the ingredients, secure the top, shake vigorously, then strain into a glass. Ten seconds shaking is enough for most drinks, but for drinks that use thick ingredients such as syrups or crèmes you should double the time.

A squeaky clean drink.

shampoo

30 ml (1 oz) gin
15 ml (1/2 oz) lemon juice
dash of Pernod
dash of blue curaçao
chilled champagne
lemon twist

Build the gin, lemon juice, Pernod and curaçao in a champagne flute. Top up with champagne. Garnish with a twist of lemon.

Bartender's tip

Pernod is a brand of French spirit flavoured with liquorice and aniseed.

A precocious cocktail for the non-drinker.

shirley temple

ice cubes	Fill a highball glass one-third full of ice, then
good dash of grenadine	add the grenadine and ginger ale. Garnish
ginger ale	with cherries and serve with a straw and a
maraschino cherries	swizzle stick.

A wonderful combo of sweet and sour flavours: two parts strong, one part sweet and one part sour.

sidecar

ice cubes	Half-fill a cocktail shaker with ice. Pour in
30 ml (1 oz) cognac	the cognac, Cointreau and lemon juice, then
15 ml (1/2 oz) Cointreau	shake well. Strain into a cocktail glass.
15 ml (1/2 oz) lemon juice	
Bartender's tip	A Sidecar is often prepared using brandy
	instead of cognac.

Distilled from the kiss of a platinum blonde, the curve of an hourglass figure and the sound of Frank Sinatra.

silk stocking

ice cubes
30 ml (1 oz) butterscotch schnapps
15 ml (1/2 oz) advocaat
15 ml (1/2 oz) white crème de cacao
30 ml (1 oz) cream
white chocolate shards

Half-fill a cocktail shaker with ice. Pour in the butterscotch schnapps, advocaat, crème de cacao and cream. Shake well and strain into a chilled martini glass. Garnish with shards of white chocolate.

Not quite a silver bullet, but still icy cold and sleek. It's just the bubbles that soften the edges.

silver fizz

ice cubes
45 ml (1 1/2 oz) gin
30 ml (1 oz) lemon juice
1 teaspoon caster sugar
half an egg white
soda water
lemon wedge

Half-fill a cocktail shaker with ice. Pour in the gin, lemon juice, sugar and egg white, then shake well until frothy. Strain into a highball glass, half-filled with ice, then top up with soda water. Garnish with a small wedge of lemon.

Invented at the Raffles hotel in Singapore in 1915, the Singapore sling still evokes days of tropical ease.

singapore sling

ice cubes
30 ml (1 oz) gin
10 ml (1/4 oz) cherry brandy
15 ml (1/2 oz) lemon juice
soda water
maraschino cherry

Half-fill a cocktail shaker with ice. Pour in the gin, cherry brandy and lemon juice, then shake well. Strain into a highball glass and top up with soda water. Garnish with a cherry and a cocktail umbrella.

The tantric cocktail — take it nice and slow.

slow comfortable screw

ice cubes
30 ml (1 oz) vodka
15 ml (1/2 oz) gin
15 ml (1/2 oz) Southern Comfort
orange juice
orange twist

Three-quarters fill a highball glass with ice. Pour in the vodka, gin and Southern Comfort. Stir, then top up with orange juice. Garnish with a twist of orange.

Some drinks can be enjoyed all year round, but this isn't one of them. It's summer in a glass.

splice

crushed ice
30 ml (1 oz) melon liqueur
30 ml (1 oz) Cointreau
15 ml (1/2 oz) Malibu
100 ml (31/2 oz) pineapple juice
60 ml (2 oz) cream
pineapple wedge
melon ball

Combine the ice, melon liqueur, Cointreau, Malibu, pineapple juice and cream in a blender and blend well. Pour into a large goblet. Garnish with a wedge of pineapple and a melon ball and serve with a straw.

sours

The sour formula is built around three flavours: lemon or lime juice, sweetener and liquor. There is no rule about the ratio of sweet to sour, but the sour flavour should dominate. Traditionally, sours were prepared in a cocktail shaker, but times have changed and they are now usually made in a blender. Sours are usually served in their own glass, a sour glass, which is similar to a champagne flute, but with a shorter stem. They can also be served on the rocks in an old-fashioned glass.

Pleasure and pain.

stinger

crushed ice or ice cubes
45 ml (1¹/2 oz) brandy
20 ml (¹/2 oz) white crème de menthe

Half-fill a small highball glass or an old-fashioned glass with ice. Pour over the brandy and crème de menthe, then stir well.

No, it's not afternoon tea time ... even better, it's cocktail time!

strawberries and cream

15 ml (1/2 oz) strawberry liqueur
30 ml (1 oz) Tia Maria
30 ml (1 oz) Irish cream
30 ml (1 oz) cream
3 fresh ripe strawberries
1 cup crushed ice
strawberries

Pour the strawberry liqueur, Tia Maria, Irish cream and cream into a blender, and add the strawberries. Blend until smooth, then add the ice and blend until the ice is slushy. Pour into a sugar-frosted cocktail glass, then garnish with fresh strawberries on a cocktail stick.

stirring cocktails

Some cocktails would become murky if shaken so, to keep them crisp and clean, they are stirred in a mixing glass or jug. A jug is easier because of its size — if you use a glass, watch out for spills and splashes. Put about six ice cubes in a mixing jug or glass and stir with a long bar spoon. Pour the liquid out, leaving the ice behind.

It's hard to go past a strawberry daiquiri at the height of summer.

strawberry daiquiri

45 ml (1¹/2 oz) white rum
15 ml (¹/2 oz) strawberry liqueur
15 ml (¹/2 oz) lime juice
6 strawberries
1 cup crushed ice

Combine the rum, strawberry liqueur, lime juice, strawberries and ice in a blender. Blend until well mixed. Pour into a large goblet. Serve with a short straw.

Bartender's tip

When you're entertaining a large group, blend up quantities of the daiquiri mixture and freeze it until an hour before your guests are due.

A drink that takes the strawberry garnish one step further.

strawberry flapper

4 hulled strawberries
4 ice cubes
15 ml (1/2 oz) strawberry liqueur
chilled champagne

Combine the strawberries, ice cubes and strawberry liqueur in a blender, and blend until smooth. Half-fill a champagne flute with the strawberry mixture and then slowly top up with champagne.

Jelly shots may not be strictly traditional, but they add a certain quirkiness to any summer cocktail party.

strawberry jelly shot

1 gelatine leaf
20 ml (1/2 oz) lemon juice
80 ml (2 1/2 oz) strawberry liqueur
3 strawberries

Soak the gelatine in cold water. Heat the lemon juice and 30 ml (1 oz) water until just hot. Squeeze the liquid out of the gelatine, add to the lemon mixture and stir until dissolved. Cool, then stir in the strawberry liqueur. Place half a strawberry into each of six shot glasses, then pour in the strawberry mixture. Refrigerate for 3 hours, or until set. Makes six.

Instead of the usual salt rim, try a combination of salt and sugar — use about one-third sugar to salt.

strawberry margarita

crushed ice	Combine the ice, tequila, strawberry liqueur, Cointreau, lime juice cordial and lemon juice in a blender and blend well. Pour into a salt-frosted cocktail glass. Garnish with half a strawberry and a slice of lemon.
30 ml (1 oz) tequila	
30 ml (1 oz) strawberry liqueur	
15 ml (1/2 oz) Cointreau	
30 ml (1 oz) lime juice cordial	
30 ml (1 oz) lemon juice	
strawberry half	
lemon slice	

Bartender's tip   Use good-quality lime juice cordial.

There are two versions of this drink — one with champagne and this refreshing one using watermelon juice.

suzy wong

ice cubes
45 ml (1¹/₂ oz) lemon-flavoured vodka
1 teaspoon lime juice
1 teaspoon sugar syrup
45 ml (1¹/₂ oz) watermelon juice
lime twist

Fill a mixing glass with ice. Pour in the vodka, lime juice, sugar syrup and watermelon juice. Stir, then strain into a chilled martini glass and garnish with a twist of lime.

Bartender's tip

Watermelon juice doesn't keep, so prepare it just before you need it.

While some are obsessed with the driest possible martini, for others a sweet martini is a thing of beauty.

sweet martini

ice cubes
45 ml (1¹/₂ oz) gin
10 ml (¹/₄ oz) vermouth rosso
olive

Fill a mixing glass at least two-thirds full of ice. Pour in the gin and vermouth and stir gently. Strain into a chilled martini glass. Garnish with an olive.

tequila

Tequila is a spirit distilled from the blue agave plant (a succulent). The origins of tequila lie in blending ancient Aztec culture and Spanish settlers' knowledge of distillation techniques. Tequila is now considered the spirit of Mexico and is governed by strict laws to protect its good name.

Mexico's magical spirit, with just a dash of sweetness to help it slide down.

tequila slammer

30 ml (1 oz) tequila
15 ml (1/2 oz) ginger ale or lemonade

Pour the tequila into a shot glass, then add the ginger ale or lemonade.

The sunrise glow of this drink is created by letting the grenadine settle to the bottom of the glass.

tequila sunrise

ice cubes
30 ml (1 oz) tequila
orange juice
1 teaspoon grenadine
orange twist

Half-fill a highball glass with ice. Pour in the tequila and top up with orange juice. Add the grenadine by carefully pouring it over the back of a spoon. Garnish with a twist of orange.

To keep the silvery perfection of a martini, use white tequila.

tequini

ice cubes	Half-fill a mixing glass with ice. Pour in the
45 ml (1½ oz) white tequila	tequila and vermouth. Stir, then strain into a
15 ml (½ oz) dry vermouth	chilled martini glass and garnish with a twist
lemon twist	of lemon.
Bartender's tip	Some versions of this drink add a dash of
	Angostura bitters and rub the lemon twist
	around the rim of the glass.

Tasteless name for a tasty drink.

test-tube baby

15 ml (¹/2 oz) amaretto 15 ml (¹/2 oz) tequila 2 drops of Irish cream	Pour the amaretto into a shot glass. Pour the tequila over the back of a teaspoon to layer. Add the Irish cream.
Bartender's tip	Some bars serve this drink in a test tube. If you're doing the same, err on the side of caution and use new test tubes.

One of the most creamy and lavish of all drinks, it somehow manages to escape being cloying.

toblerone

1 teaspoon honey
15 ml (1/2 oz) chocolate syrup
pinch of finely chopped hazelnuts
ice cubes
30 ml (1 oz) Frangelico
15 ml (1/2 oz) Irish cream
15 ml (1/2 oz) Tia Maria
15 ml (1/2 oz) creamy chocolate liqueur
60 ml (2 oz) cream
shaved chocolate

Drizzle the honey and 1 teaspoon chocolate syrup down the sides of a large, chilled martini glass, and sprinkle with chopped hazelnuts. Chill. Half-fill a cocktail shaker with ice. Pour in the Frangelico, Irish cream, Tia Maria, chocolate liqueur and cream, shake well and strain into the prepared martini glass. Garnish with shaved chocolate.

A drink so good that it gets its own special glass.

tom collins

ice cubes
30 ml (1 oz) gin
15 ml (1/2 oz) lemon juice
15 ml (1/2 oz) sugar syrup
soda water
maraschino cherry

Half-fill a collins glass or highball glass with ice. Pour in the gin, lemon juice and sugar syrup. Stir well and top up with soda water. Garnish with a cherry.

Yes, no, maybe ...

traffic lights

15 ml (1/2 oz) banana liqueur
15 ml (1/2 oz) strawberry liqueur
15 ml (1/2 oz) melon liqueur

Pour the banana liqueur into a shot glass. Slowly pour the strawberry liqueur into the glass over the back of a teaspoon to layer. Repeat with melon liqueur to form three distinct layers.

As far as non-alcoholic cocktails go, this one has serious cachet.

virgin mary

2 teaspoons celery salt
1 teaspoon black pepper
ice cubes
125 ml (4 oz) tomato juice
15 ml (1/2 oz) lemon juice
1 teaspoon Worcestershire sauce
dash of Tabasco sauce
celery stick

Frost the rim of a large goblet with combined celery salt and pepper. Half-fill a cocktail shaker with ice. Pour in the tomato juice, lemon juice, Worcestershire sauce and Tabasco and shake well. Strain into a goblet, then garnish with a stick of celery.

vodka

Vodka is made by fermenting and then distilling the simple sugars from a mash of pale grain or vegetable matter. Rye and wheat are the classic grains for vodka. Because it is neutral in flavour, vodka is often flavoured with fruits, herbs and spices — lemon vodka and pepper vodka are both popular flavoured vodkas. Unlike other liquors, such as whisky and gin, vodka is generally not aged for long.

James Bond had it wrong — it should be stirred, not shaken.

vodkatini

ice cubes
80 ml (2¹/₂ oz) vodka
15 ml (¹/₂ oz) dry vermouth
lemon twist

Half-fill a mixing glass with ice. Pour in the vodka and vermouth and stir. Strain into a chilled martini glass and garnish with a twist of lemon.

Cool down with a refreshing watermelon cocktail.

watermelon cocktail

ice cubes	Half-fill a highball glass with ice. Pour in the
1 teaspoon lime juice	lime juice, gin and watermelon liqueur. Top
30 ml (1 oz) gin	up with watermelon juice, stir and garnish
15 ml (^{1}/2 oz) watermelon liqueur	with a slice of lime.
watermelon juice	
lime slice	

Bartender's tip	To make watermelon juice, either use a juicer,
	or remove the rind and seeds and process the
	flesh in a food processor. Strain before using.

The interplay of sour, sweet and strong flavours sings in the mouth.

whisky sour

ice cubes
45 ml (1¹/2 oz) Scotch whisky
30 ml (1 oz) lemon juice
15 ml (¹/2 oz) sugar syrup
lemon wedge
maraschino cherry

Half-fill a cocktail shaker with ice. Pour in the whisky, lemon juice and sugar syrup, then shake well. Strain into a sour glass or small wine glass and garnish with a wedge of lemon and a cherry.

Fashion tip: this elegant aperitif looks particularly striking against an all-black ensemble.

white lady

ice cubes	Half-fill a cocktail shaker with ice. Pour in the
30 ml (1 oz) gin	gin, Cointreau, lemon juice and egg white,
15 ml ($^1/_2$ oz) Cointreau	then shake well. Strain into a cocktail glass.
15 ml ($^1/_2$ oz) lemon juice	
dash of egg white (optional)	

whisky

The four major producers of this grain-based spirit are Scotland, Ireland, the United States and Canada. With so many countries producing it, several different types of whisky have developed. Of these, the main ones are Scotch (blended or malt), Irish, Canadian, American (bourbon, rye and Tennessee) and Japanese. Whisky is aged (often for long periods) in barrels. It is this aging that softens and smoothes the taste and provides the aromatic flavour.

It's hard to imagine Russians mixing their beloved vodka with cream, but for the rest of us this creamy drink is a delight.

white russian

ice cubes	Half-fill an old-fashioned glass with ice. Pour
45 ml (1 1/2 oz) vodka	over the vodka and Kahlúa, then float the
30 ml (1 oz) Kahlúa	cream across the top by carefully pouring it
20 ml (1/2 oz) cream	over the back of a teaspoon.

The tartness of cranberry tamed by the sweetness of peach.

WOO WOO

ice cubes
lime wedge
60 ml (2 oz) vodka
15 ml ($1/2$ oz) peach schnapps
cranberry juice

Half-fill a cocktail shaker with ice. Squeeze the lime wedge into the shaker, and add the vodka and peach schnapps. Shake, then strain into an old-fashioned glass half-filled with ice. Add the squeezed lime wedge to the glass and top up with cranberry juice.

Once you've mastered your ABCs, move onto an XYZ.

xyz

ice cubes	Half-fill a cocktail shaker with ice. Pour in
30 ml (1 oz) dark rum	the rum, Cointreau and lemon juice, then
15 ml (1/2 oz) Cointreau	shake well. Strain into a martini or cocktail
15 ml (1/2 oz) lemon juice	glass and garnish with a cherry.
maraschino cherry	

Beware — this drink is potent and might wake the dead.

zombie

ice cubes
30 ml (1 oz) white rum
30 ml (1 oz) dark rum
30 ml (1 oz) overproof rum
15 ml (1/2 oz) apricot brandy
15 ml (1/2oz) cherry brandy
60 ml (2 oz) orange juice
15 ml (1/2 oz) lime juice
fresh fruit

Half-fill a cocktail shaker with ice. Pour in the white rum, dark rum, overproof rum, apricot brandy, cherry brandy, orange juice and lime juice, then shake well. Half-fill a highball glass with ice and then strain into the glass. Garnish with fresh fruit and serve with a straw.

drink finder

The drink finder is arranged so that you can find your drink by looking under the base spirit, by which we mean the most dominant liquor in a drink. If a drink has equal quantities of several of these spirits it will be listed under each spirit. We've included only the major liquors in this list: brandy, cachaça, Campari, gin, rum, tequila, vodka and whisky.

If you have a particular occasion in mind, look under the drink categories. For example, if you want a pre-dinner drink, go straight to the list of aperitifs. Or, if you want a little something before bed, look under digestifs. The major drink categories that we've included are aperitifs, champagne and wine cocktails, coladas, collinses, daiquiris, digestifs, eggnogs/flips, fizzes, highballs, jelly shots, juleps, margaritas, martinis (and variations), mocktails, pick-me-ups, punches, shooters and sours. Thus, many cocktails appear in two or more categories.

aperitifs

brandy drinks

digestifs

eggnogs/flips

whisky drinks